DEAR,

May the Almighty bless you and your family with his blessing.

Why We Love Our Prophet Muhammad ﷺ?
The Short Seerah of Prophet Muhammad ﷺ for Kids

ISBN: 978-1-990544-88-0

ARABIA BEFORE ISLAM

Before the advent of Islam, the condition of a common man was grave in the region. It was a tribal society where buying and selling slaves was a common activity. It was a society where inter-tribal fighting was common, even for a meagre reason.

The Arab society was made up of different tribes and there was no proper government. They choose the tribal chiefs who had the power to decide on a tribal issue. The chief can only be selected on the basis of family history and/or personality traits. A single regular government was lacking.

Arab culture was very rich because the storytelling was very common in Arabia. This is the main reason they called non-Arabs fools. They were very good at poetry and proud of their Arabic language and culture. Despite all this, social conditions in Arabia were so bad that caravan theft was considered a common practice among the Arab people. They sold and bought slaves like animals, and the social status of slaves was nothing more than that of animals. It was a purely male-dominated society in which being the father of a daughter was considered a disgrace. Stealing, drinking and gambling were common.

Most of the Arabs at that time were not able to read and write. Umar bin Khattab[(R.A)], the second caliph of the Muslims, was one of those who could read and write before the advent of Islam.

Due to the inter-tribal wars, the economic situation was not flourishing in the region. They used to send commercial caravans to other nearby areas as no industry was developed in the peninsular region. However, the Jewish community was in good shape. Most of the arable land was under their occupation.

At a time when everything was in its worst state such as education, political system, economic conditions, social conditions, and law and order, etc. Allah Almighty sent the last

Prophet, Prophet Muhammad ﷺ as a revolutionary for all humankind. It was a miracle in the history of mankind that the entire situation on the Arabian Peninsula flipped in less than hundred years. Our Prophet ﷺ transformed the status of the people of Arabia from slaves to the leaders of the entire region. The mindset of Arabs changed from cruelty to being compassionate.

"Indeed, in the Messenger of Allah you have an excellent example," (Surah Ahzab, V:21)

EARLY LIFE OF ALLAH's MESSENGER ﷺ AND HIS RELATIONSHIP WITH THE COMMUNITY

Prophet Muhammad ﷺ was born into a famous and pious Quraish tribe known as 'the Banu Hashim' in Makkah city. His father's name is Abdullah(R.A), who died almost six months before Prophet Muhammad's ﷺ birth. Her mother's name was Syeda Amina(R.A), who belongs to the Banu Zuhrah clan of the Quraish tribe. According to Arab tradition, Prophet Muhammad ﷺ sent to live with a milk mother, Syeda Halimah(R.A), as life in the desert was considered healthier for babies.

At six years of age, he was reunited with his mother, Syeda Aminah(R.A), who took him to visit her relatives in Yathrib city (later called Medina). Upon their return to Makkah a month later, accompanied by her slave Umm Ayman, Aminah(R.A) fell ill. She passed away on this journey and was buried in the village of Abwa'. After that, he was raised by his paternal grandfather, Abd al-Muttalib, until 'upon his death when Prophet Muhammad ﷺ was eight

years old. He then came into the care of his uncle Abu Talib, who was elected the new leader of Banu Hashim.

While still in his teens, Prophet Muhammad ﷺ accompanied his uncle on trading journeys to Syria, gaining experience in commercial trade, which was the only career open to him as an orphan. Islamic tradition states that when Prophet Muhammad ﷺ was either nine or twelve while accompanying a caravan to Syria he met a Christian monk or hermit named Bahira, who is said to have foreseen his career as a Prophet of Allah(S.W.T).

Due to his upright character during this time, he acquired the nickname "al-Amin," meaning "faithful, trustworthy," and "al-Sadiq," meaning "truthful."

All the tribes of Makkah, even his enemies during the time of his preaching of Islam, trust him more than any other person and used to handover their precious kinds of stuff for safekeeping as they knew that our Holy Prophet ﷺ would never embezzle them. Also, they knew that Prophet Muhammad ﷺ would never lie in any matter. This is the first lesson to all Muslims to uplift their characters in society as true believers of Islam.

"Indeed, Allah has done the believers a ˹great˺ favour by raising a messenger from among them—reciting to them His revelations, purifying them, and teaching them the Book and wisdom. For indeed they had previously been clearly astray."
(Surah Aal-e-Imran, V:164)

PROPHET MUHAMMAD ﷺ AS A MERCY FOR ALL

"We have sent you ˹O Prophet˺ only as a mercy for the whole world."
(Surah Al-Anbya, V:107)

As part of His endearing love for His creations, Allah(S.W.T) bestowed us with the love of His beloved messenger, Prophet Muhammad ﷺ. The Messenger of Allah ﷺ lived among us and showed us the path of attaining eternal love. He did not only teach us how to love our Creator but also how to love other creations. He is the light that guided the hearts and brightens the inner darkness. He is created as the epitome of mercy and the paragon of virtues.

THE INCIDENT OF TAIF VALLEY

During the first ten years of preaching Islam, Makkah had proved inhospitable to our Holy Prophet ﷺ and his Companions(R.A). It occurred to the Rasulallah ﷺ that he ought, perhaps to try to preach the true faith in some other city. The nearest city was Ta'if, a lush town of green palm trees, fruits and vegetables, 50 miles in the south-east of Makkah. Zayd bin Haritha(R.A) went with him.

In Ta'if, the Messenger of Allah ﷺ, called on the three chiefs of the local tribes and invited them to abandon their worship of idols, to acknowledge the Oneness of Allah, to throwaway man-made distinctions of high and low, and to believe in the equality and brotherhood of all.

The chiefs of Ta'if were a conceited and arrogant crew, and they did not want even to listen to the Prophet ﷺ. They greeted him with mockery and ridicule and set upon him the loafers and the hooligans of the city. They pelted him and Zayd with clods and rocks.

Wounded and covered with blood, our dear Prophet ﷺ came out of Ta'if. In the face of this misery, Angel Jibrael(A.S) was sent and presented him with an option: have the whole town be destroyed, by God's will, for such arrogance and hatefulness, "If you say I will grind these people between two mountains and no one will be left behind."

He could have done it. He could have asked that this valley of cruel people be crushed. But he didn't.

"No," he told the Angel. "Don't destroy the people of Taif." Instead, he prayed for their salvation. In extreme sorrow, the Holy Prophet ﷺ said, "I am an example of kindness. I don't want to take revenge. Their offspring will surely accept Islam."

As Allah(S.W.T) revealed in the Qur'an,

> "We have sent you ˹O Prophet˺ only as a mercy for the whole world."
> (Surah Al-Anbya, V:107)

That is just one of many instances of how our Holy Prophet ﷺ, who God describes as a "mercy for everyone", dealt with those who opposed him. The visit of Ta'if Valley is one example in the life of the Holy Prophet ﷺ who faced constant death threats and attempts on his life, abuse and humiliation at the hands of those threatened by his simple but profound message: there is no god but Allah and Muhammad ﷺ is His Slave and Messenger.

THE PEACEFUL VICTORY OF MAKKAH

Another well-known example of the kindness and mercy of Rasulallah ﷺ is during the peaceful takeover of Makkah by the Muslims. Here, too, the Holy Prophet ﷺ demonstrated exemplary behaviour. It is common human nature, when in a position of power or when the opportunity presents itself, people are known for abusing their authority and punishing their enemies brutally. But at that time, when he could have easily destroyed his worst enemies, our Holy Prophet ﷺ showed remarkable restraint. This is even more significant given the culture of vicious tribal rivalry practised at the time.

Prophet Muhammad ﷺ is a mercy to all human beings, regardless of their religious, racial, cultural or ethnic background. We, as his followers, must live and spread this message today at a time when hatefulness and ugliness towards each other have become the norm.

KINDNESS TOWARDS SERVANTS

Islam is a complete code of life. The followers of Islam are given explicit instructions on how to treat servants, workers, and the help. There are many examples that show the kindness and gentleness of the Holy Prophet ﷺ towards their servants. Anas b. Malik[R.A] was the Prophet's ﷺ personal servant for ten years until he passed away in Makkah. Anas[R.A] had a great love for the Holy Prophet ﷺ and took great joy and pride in attending to his needs. According to him, Rasulallah ﷺ not once strike or even reprimand him. He would wake up before everyone else in the mornings and go to the Prophet's ﷺ mosque to take care of his needs and wishes.

Anas[R.A] said, "I served the Holy Prophet ﷺ at home and on journeys. By Allah, he never said to me for anything which I did: 'Why have you done this?' or for anything which I did not do: 'Why have you not done this?'" (Sahih Bukhari and Muslim)

Prophet Muhammad ﷺ said, "They (servants) are only your brothers. Allah has placed them in your care. So, whoever has a brother under his care, then feed him from what you eat, clothe him with what you clothe yourself. Not overburden him with that which he cannot bear. And if you overburden him, then lend him a hand." This Hadith applies also to female servants of course.

One companion, Abu Dharr[R.A], upon hearing the Prophet's ﷺ words, never again spoke harshly to a slave or servant. Abu Dharr[R.A] was then very careful to treat the servant as he would treat his own children. He was seen walking in the markets with his servant, and the servant boy was wearing the exact same ornament on his clothes that Abu Dharr[R.A] himself was wearing. This is the teaching of our Holy Prophet ﷺ in the hostile environment of Makkah of that time.

Empathy is very encouraged in Islam. Prophet Muhammad ﷺ said, "When your servant prepares food for you and lays it for you — while he has suffered the inconvenience of heat and smoke when cooking — you should ask him to sit down and share the meal."

As for delaying wages, which is not uncommon today, that is an injustice and is impermissible in Islam. Prophet Muhammad ﷺ instructed, "Pay the labourer his wages before his sweat dries."

Imagine! A housemaid who has scrubbed, cleaned, washed, ironed, cooked, and toiled, should see the fruits of her labour as she wipes her brow after a day or week or month of hard work — whichever time period was agreed upon between the employer and employee. The salary of her hard work is the only thing that sustains her daily errands, and that is why she is out of her home, working for others. The Holy Prophet ﷺ explains that Allah(S.W.T) on the Day of Judgment will be angry with and will be the opponent of the person who "employs a labourer and takes full work from him but does not pay him for his labour."

Once, a man came to Rasulallah ﷺ and asked, "O Prophet of Allah! To what extent should we forgive the mistakes and faults of our servants?" The Holy Prophet ﷺ remained silent and when the man repeated the question for the third time, he replied, "Seventy times a day." (Al-Tirmidhi)

None of us would ever want to go against our Lord or have His anger descend upon us. However, we are risking just that when we harm our servants.

The help we hire, just like us, will make mistakes; we are all human. The housemaid may accidentally burn a dress while ironing it, spill coffee on the rug, or break a crystal glass. Patience, pardoning, and forgiving are called for. Picture that, only after the 70th mistake that the housemaid makes in one day can we lose our patience.

The Prophet's wife, Syeda Aisha[(R.A)], said, "The Messenger of Allah ﷺ never struck a woman or a child or a servant." (Sahih Muslim)

It is unnerving how some of us actually brag about how many rules they have imposed on their servants. Islam is not just what we write on our passports in the space for 'Religion'. Islam is a belief held in the heart, enforced by the words and manner in which we speak, and finally, it controls the actions of our entire body; our limbs, eyes, what we eat, and what we listen to.

Even in today's modern world, we have all heard stories of housemaids working without rest until after midnight and rising early with the sun, or those working for months on without pay; their wages being withheld from them. A servant accidentally broke an expensive vase and was forced to repay the family for the vase; which was equivalent to half of his/her monthly salary. Worse yet, we read shocking reports of domestic workers brutally beaten by their employers.

It is high time to absorb all these sayings of our Holy Prophet ﷺ and implement them in our daily lives. This is the culture that our Prophet ﷺ taught us fourteen hundred years ago when no college or university was teaching them moral and ethical values. All our domestic helpers have a right to be treated with mercy, compassion, kindness, and to be paid their wages on time.

KINDNESS TOWARDS CHILDREN

The Prophet ﷺ said, "Indeed among the believers with the most complete faith is the one who is the best in conduct and the most kind to his family." (Tirmizi)

Needless to say, the Prophet's ﷺ innate nature of being a mercy for all of God's creations is certain. His mercy is unparalleled and indeed, his treatment of children, and not just for his own family, is an example to us all. For example, upon arriving in Medinah, the Prophet Muhammad ﷺ was received by the elite people of Medinah along with other men and women who were eagerly waiting for his blessed arrival. Among the huge crowd that lined up to welcome the long-awaited Messenger of Allah ﷺ, were the children of Medinah who broke out in singing and praising him. Rasulallah ﷺ turned towards them smiling and gave them his undivided attention. He went up to them with a smile on his face and asked them, "Do you love me?" The children out of joy and excitement said, "Yes, yes! We love and respect you, O Messenger of Allah ﷺ." The Prophet replied, "And I also love you all." The children were delighted!

The Holy Prophet ﷺ would kiss and embrace children often, as an expression of his tender, love and mercy towards them. In a hadith about children, Abu Huraira[R.A] reported that al-Aqra' bin Habis saw Allah's Messenger ﷺ kissing Hasan Ibn Ali[A.S]. He said: "I have ten children, but I have never kissed any of them," Whereupon Allah's Messenger ﷺ said: "He who does not show mercy (towards his children), no mercy would be shown to him." (Muslim)

It is narrated by the mother of the believers, Syeda Aisha Siddiqua[R.A], that Whenever Rasulallah ﷺ visited by his youngest daughter, Syeda Fatimah[S.A], he would stand to welcome her when she entered the room, take her by the hand, kiss her and make her sit where he was sitting. Conversely, she would do the same when he visited her. These beautiful acts, though simple, show the profound love and respect the father and daughter held for each other. Consider this behaviour in the era when the newly born daughters were buried alive only for the sake of avoiding the embarrassment of the community.

Our Holy Prophet ﷺ would also take an active interest in children's lives, despite his busy schedule. For example, Anas bin Malik(R.A) said: "The Messenger of Allah ﷺ used to come to visit us. I had a younger brother who was called Abu 'Umair by nickname (kunyah). He had a sparrow which he played with, but it died. So, one day, Rasulallah ﷺ came to see him and saw him grieving. He asked: 'What is the matter with him?' The people replied: 'His sparrow has died.' Rasulallah ﷺ then said: 'Oh Abu 'Umair! What has happened to the little sparrow?'" (Abu Daud). In this hadith, we see the example of Prophet Muhammad ﷺ who goes out of his way to share the grief of a young child, whereas many adults would brush away such a seemingly insignificant matter. This kind of relationship can build trust, open communication, and validation for the child. Our Holy Prophet ﷺ has taught us how to treat kids well, and how to express the love and joy.

Prophet Muhammad ﷺ used to care for orphans and he used to ask his companions to protect them and to treat them well. He also showed the merits that come from this. Al-Bukhari narrated that Prophet Muhammad ﷺ said: "I and the custodian of an orphan are like this (together) in Paradise", and he joined his forefinger and middle finger together. Another saying related to the orphan is; Prophet Muhammad ﷺ said: "The best Muslim house is one in which an orphan is well treated, and the worst Muslim house is one in which an orphan is badly treated." These Prophetic sayings show clearly that if someone takes good care of an orphan, he is sure to enter paradise.

Rasulallah ﷺ was a role model in caring for children in a society where just loving the children was an issue of the ego. He ﷺ taught us how to treat them and how to express love and joy for the gift of having them. It is our obligation to learn how best to treat children and to incorporate these teachings in our own life.

KINDNESS TO THE POOR

One of the great reforms that Prophet Muhammad ﷺ brought was the rights of the poors and treatment towards them. Prior to the advent of Islam, pagan Arabs used to disregard the poor. They would look down on them, and could care less about them; the poor people were basically an insignificant portion of society. However so, with the teachings of our Holy Prophet ﷺ, all that changed. Muslims were now obliged to look after the poor and were required to spend their wealth to help out the poor.

To become closer to Allah(S.W.T), we look to the Messenger of Allah ﷺ as a guide, teacher and example of what a good Muslim should be. So, on our path towards Allah, let us look at Rasulallah ﷺ for inspiration on how to help our brothers and sisters in need around us. The Holy Prophet ﷺ said, "Blessed is the wealth of the Muslim, from which he gives to the poor, the orphan and the traveller." (Muslim)

Humble, modest and loving, Prophet Muhammad ﷺ was known for his generosity. As 'the most generous of all the people...' (Bukhari), the Holy Prophet ﷺ continuously encouraged his followers to help others, calling upon Muslims to support their families, neighbours, communities and the wider ummah. Emphasising the importance of charity, Rasulallah ﷺ said:

"Generosity is near to Allah, near to Paradise, near to the people, and far from the Hellfire..." (Tirmidhi)

As Muslims, we are urged to help ensure the poor and needy do not go hungry especially people around us, like our next-door neighbours. As we look to the example of the Holy Prophet ﷺ for guidance in fulfilling our duties as Muslims, we are reminded of the need to help others who lack even the daily essentials we enjoy but may take for granted.

Prophet Muhammad ﷺ said:

"He is not a Muslim whose stomach is full while his neighbour goes hungry." (Muslim)

"None of you have faith until you love for your neighbour what you love for yourself." (Muslim)

"Whenever a beggar came to Allah's Apostle ﷺ or he was asked for something, he ﷺ used to say (to his companions), "Help and recommend him and you will receive the reward for it." (Sahih Al-Bukhari; Volume 2, Book 24, Number 512)

In another hadith, The Holy Prophet ﷺ said: "The one who looks after a widow or a poor person is like him who performs prayers all the night and fasts all the day." (Sahih Al-Bukhari; Volume 7, Book 64, Number 265)

Rasulallah ﷺ once said to his wife: "Ayesha(R.A)! Never turn a poor man away from your door empty-handed. O Ayesha! Love the poor, bring them closer to you and Allah will bring you closer to Him."

Islam does not prohibit or discourage the acquisition of wealth but insists that it is acquired legally through honest means and that part of it goes to the poor. One of the pillars of Islam is 'Zakah'; a compulsory act for rich people of giving a portion of wealth to the poor. The Holy Prophet ﷺ ordered Muslims to treat the poor with kindness and to help them with alms, zakat, and other ways.

Not only the Holy Prophet ﷺ encourages others to take care of poors but also, he himself was very concerned for them.

A man from Medina, Ibaad Ibn Sharjil, was once starving. He went into a private orchard and picked some fruits. The owner of the garden gave him a strong blow and stripped off his clothes. The poor man appealed to the Holy Prophet ﷺ, who rebuked the owner saying: "This man was unaware, you should have ousted his unawareness; He was hungry, you should have fed him." The poor man's clothes were restored and, also, he was given grain. [Abu Daawood]

One debtor, Jaabir ibn Abdullaah(R.A) was harassed by his creditor because he could not pay his debt due to the failure of his date harvest. The Holy Prophet ﷺ went with Jaabir to the creditor's house and said to him to give Jaabir more time, but the creditor was unwilling. The Holy Prophet ﷺ then went to the oasis and, having seen for himself that the harvest was really bad, he again approached the creditor with no better result. He then rested for a while and approached the creditor for the third time, but the creditor stood firm. The Holy Prophet ﷺ returned to the garden and asked Jaabir to pluck the dates. As Allah(S.W.T) willed, the collection not only sufficed to clear the dues but left something to spare. [Al-Bukhari]

Rasulallah's ﷺ love for the poor was so deep that he used to pray: "O Allah, keep me poor in my life and in my death, and raise me in resurrection among the poor." [An-Nasaa'ee]

Thus, one can see the very high value and importance that Islam attaches to helping and looking after the poor. This teaching is a major incentive and motivation for the people to take care, and to look after the poor. Indeed, what a great reform the Prophet Muhammad (s.a.w.w.) brought! Now if all of us could follow these teachings in regards to the poor people around us, then our society would be a much better place!

CARING FOR ANIMALS AND BIRDS

Prophet Muhammad ﷺ is an embodiment of mercy; he expressed sympathy to not only humans around him but also treated the animals with respect and compassion. He taught his followers that since animals are part of God's creation, they should be treated with dignity. He ﷺ said, "Truly, there is a heavenly reward for every act of kindness done to a living creature."

Humans were created by Allah, the Almighty, to be custodians and guardians of the Earth. Prophet Muhammad s.a.w. was always gentle with other creations.

Abu Huraira reported Allah's Messenger ﷺ as saying:

A person suffered from intense thirst while on a journey when he found a well. He climbed down into it and drank (water) and then came out and saw a dog lolling its tongue on account of thirst and eating the moistened earth. The person said: This dog has suffered from thirst as I had suffered from it. He climbed down into the well, filled his shoe with water, then caught it in his mouth until he climbed up and made the dog drink it. So, Allah appreciated this act of his and pardoned him. Then (the Companions around him) said: Allah's Messenger, is there for us a reward even for (serving) such animals? He said: Yes, there is a reward for service to every living animal. (Sahih Muslim 2244)

Even though we regard some animals as impure, Muslims are expected to respect and handle them with love and mercy. For instance, in dealing with dogs, the Holy Prophet ﷺ did not teach us to hate them. In fact, in the above Hadith, he ﷺ told us about the merits of feeding any animal.

The traditions of the Prophet Muhammad ﷺ remind us that humanity was made the guardian of God's creation on this earth. Treating animals with kindness and compassion is one of those responsibilities. It is clear from the words and deeds of Rasulallah ﷺ that it is not only completely unacceptable to inflict pain and suffering on defenceless creatures, but we will also be accountable to God for such acts. Killing without need- that is killing for fun- is not permissible. Islam expects humanity to treat all living things - birds, marine animals and insects, with dignity.

The Messenger of Allah ﷺ gave constant advice to the people to show kindness to all the creatures. He prohibited the practice of cutting off horses' tails and manes, marking animals at any weak spots, and keeping horses unnecessarily saddled. [Muslim] The Messenger of Allah ﷺ once passed by a camel that was so scrawny that its back had almost reached its stomach. He said, "Fear Allah in these beasts who cannot speak." (Abu Dawud)

All living creatures were put on this earth by God for our benefit. They are not at the same level as human beings but neither should they be treated cruelly. It is humankind's responsibility to see that they have been provided with sufficient food, water, and shelter. Living creatures must not be overburdened, abused, or tortured and doing so will surely result in God's just punishment. If Rasulallah ﷺ saw that any animal was overloaded or sick, he would speak softly to the owner and say, "Fear God in your dealings with animals." (Abu Dawud)

However, refraining from physical abuse is not enough. It is just as important to avoid mental cruelty. Even a bird's emotional distress should be taken seriously. Once, a group of Companions were on a journey with the Messenger of Allah ﷺ, and he left them for a while. During his absence, they saw a bird with its two young, and they took the young ones from the nest. The mother bird was circling above in the air, beating its wings in grief. When the Holy Prophet ﷺ came back (and saw the bird's distress). He said, "Who has hurt the feelings of this bird by taking its young? Return them to her." (Muslim)

It is narrated that Rasulallah ﷺ said, "If someone kills a bird for a game, the bird will cry out on the Day of Judgment, 'Lord! This guy killed me in vain! He did not kill me for any useful purpose.'" (Sunan al-Nisa'i)

Narrated Ibn 'Umar(R.A): The Prophet ﷺ said: "A woman was punished on account of a cat which she held captive till it died. Hence, she entered the Hell-Fire due to (her mistreatment of) the cat. She did not feed it or give it water while she held it captive, nor did she let it out so that it may eat the things that creep on the earth." (Sunan Ibn Majah 4256)

Imagine, in pre-Islamic times, society was so cruel that a powerful man doesn't spare a mistake of a common man, and encourages harsh practices including cruelty to animals; there came a man, Our Dear Prophet ﷺ, who preached Islam (meaning peace), and condemned and forbade all such cruel practices. Allah(S.W.T) has ordained goodness and virtue in everything. For a true believer, it is very important to protect animals from undue harm.

PLANTING TREES IS RECOMMENDED BY ISLAM

As plants are also regarded as living being, Prophet Muhammad ﷺ emphasised us that we have a collective duty towards our environment. He ﷺ encouraged us to plant trees as it would benefit other creations.

Prophet Muhammad ﷺ said,

"No Muslim who plants a tree or sows seeds, and then a bird, or a person or an animal eats from it, except that this is regarded as charity." (Sahih al-Bukhari 2320)

Today, with the threats of climate change and global warming, there is a need for us to treat our environment with love and respect. We should make efforts to prevent wastage, over-reliance on single-use plastic, and make efforts not to pollute our waters and the air.

We need to inculcate our love towards the environment and make efforts to protect it from degradation and destruction.

Not only the Messenger of Allah ﷺ used to love and care for the creatures of Allah but the creature loves him too. A wonderful Hadith tells us about a date-palm tree branch that loves to be near to the Prophet of Allah ﷺ.

Narrated Jabir bin `Abdullah(R.A): The Prophet ﷺ used to stand by a tree or a date-palm on Friday. Then an Ansari woman or man said. "O Allah's Messenger ﷺ! Shall we make a pulpit for you?" He replied, "If you wish." So, they made a pulpit for him and when it was Friday, he proceeded towards the pulpit (for delivering the sermon). The datepalm cried like a child! The Prophet ﷺ descended (the pulpit) and embraced it while it continued moaning like a child being quietened. The Prophet ﷺ said, "It was crying for (missing) what it used to hear of religious knowledge given near to it." (Sahih al-Bukhari 3584)

Imam Al-Hasan Al-Basri used to cry when narrating a similar hadith and say: "O servants of Allah, the wood yearns towards the meeting of Prophet Muhammad ﷺ. Yet you have more right to look forward to meeting him."

A true believer in Allah(S.W.T) demonstrates his or her belief by respecting the entire creation, and our Prophet Muhammad's ﷺ character and teachings, is a brilliant model to follow for the modern world.

HOW SAHABA (R.A) (COMPANIONS) LOVE PROPHET MUHAMMAD ﷺ

It was narrated that Anas bin Malik said:

"The Messenger of Allah ﷺ said: 'None of you truly believes until I am more beloved to him than his child, his father and all the people.'"

Anas b. Malik reported that a desert Arab said to Allah's Messenger ﷺ: When would be the Last Hour? Allah's Messenger ﷺ said: What preparation have you made for that? Thereupon he said: The love of Allah and of His Messenger (that is my preparation for the Last Hour) (for the Day of Resurrection). Thereupon he (the Holy Prophet ﷺ) said: You would be along with one whom you love. (Sahih Muslim 2639a)

What a great tiding it is to know this. We love our Prophet Muhammad ﷺ and surely, he is the one with the highest status and best of the creations.

It has been reported on the authority of Anas b. Malik that [when the enemy got the upper hand] on the day of the Battle of Uhud, the Messenger of Allah ﷺ was left with only seven men from the Ansar and two men from the Quraish. When the enemy advanced towards him and overwhelmed him, he said: Whoso turns them away from us will attain Paradise or will be my Companion in Paradise. A man from the Ansar came forward and fought [the enemy] until he was killed. The enemy advanced and overwhelmed him again and he repeated the words: Whoso turns them away, from us will attain Paradise or will be my Companion in Paradise. A man from the Ansar came forward and fought until he was killed. This state continued until the seven Ansar were killed [one after the other]. [Muslim 19:4413]

After the martyrdom of the seventh Ansari in Uhud, two Quraishis were left guarding the Prophet ﷺ: Talha bin Ubaidullah and Sad bin Abi Waqas. These two Sahabas bravely fought the Quraish and used their own bodies as shields to protect Allah's Messenger ﷺ.

Narrated Qais: I saw Talha's paralyzed hand with which he had protected the Prophet on the day of Uhud. [Bukhari 59:392]

The Prophet ﷺ was left with Talha bin Ubaidullah and Sad bin Abi Waqas for only a few seconds before other Sahabas arrived to shield him. Abu Dujanah(R.A) made himself a shield for Allah's Messenger ﷺ. Arrows kept on striking his back yet he continued to bend over Allah's Messenger ﷺ [to protect him] and in the end, many arrows pierced his back. [Seerat ibn Hisham] Such was their love for him.

There was the woman from the family of Bani Dinar. By the end of the battle of Uhud, many of the Muslims died and the Prophet ﷺ was severely injured to the extent that news was spread that he has died when he actually did not. After the completion of the battle, certain people were sent to visit the families of those who have died in the battle and convey to them whom from their family has passed away. Among the saddest and toughest cases of all was the case of a woman from the family of Bani Dinar. It was narrated by Ibn Katheer in his book Al-Bedaayah Wan-nehaayah that the people came to her and told her about the passing of her father, brother and husband. And to their surprise, her concern and question was: "What happened to the Prophet of Allah ﷺ?" They replied: "Goodness, O mother of so and so. He, by the praise of Allah, is doing just like how you would wish." Then she requested: "Take me to where he is so I can see him". So, they pointed him out and as she spotted Prophet Muhammad ﷺ she said: "Every calamity besides losing you is bearable." SubhanAllah!

When Allah's Messenger ﷺ announced the preparation for the Battle of Tabuk and called for charities and donations, the Muslims raced to spend for the sake of Allah(S.W.T). Syeduna Uthman(R.A), for instance, who had prepared two hundred saddled camels to travel to Ash-Sham, presented them all with two hundred ounces (of gold) as charity. He also fetched a thousand dinars and cast them all into the lap of the Messenger of Allah ﷺ, who turned them over and said: "From this day on, nothing will harm Uthman(R.A) regardless of what he does." [Jami' At-Tirmidhi 2/211] Again and again Syeduna Uthman(R.A) gave till his charity reached nine hundred camels and a hundred horses, besides the money he paid.

We should compare our love to that of the great Companions of Rasulallah ﷺ. Are we ready to give up our desires and can sacrifice our beloved most things to obey the Holy Prophet ﷺ? Our desire for the company of the Messenger of Allah ﷺ in Paradise requires a firm following of Islam like his companions.

LOVE OF UMMAH

As Muslims we love our Holy Prophet ﷺ more than anyone, but do we know how much he loved us? Do we know about his great compassion? One of the greatest ways to love Prophet Muhammad ﷺ is simply by knowing how much good he has done to us out of love and care. Let's explore some Qur'anic verses and hadiths about his love and compassion for us; his Ummah.

In the noble Qur'an, Allah(S.W.T) revealed that how much Rasulallah ﷺ put his Ummah near to his heart and supplicate to Allah for our easing,

"There certainly has come to you a messenger from among yourselves. He is concerned by your suffering, anxious for your well-being, and gracious and merciful to the believers."
(Surah At-Tawbah, V:128)

Sheikh Sa'adi(a.r), a great Islamic Scholar, indicated that "this bounty is the most valuable of Allah's bounties bestowed to his worshippers: he sent them this Noble Prophet ﷺ to take them out of misguidance and protect them from punishment."

The mother of the believers, Syeda A'ishah(r.a), narrates "Once, when I saw the Prophet ﷺ in a good mood, I said to him: "O Messenger of Allah! Supplicate to Allah for me!" So, he said: "O Allah! Forgive A'ishah her past sins and her future sins, the sins which she has hidden and the sins which have been made apparent." So, I began smiling, to the point that my head fell into the lap of the Messenger of Allah out of joy. The Messenger of Allah ﷺ said to me: "Does my supplication make you happy?" I replied: "And how can your supplication not make me happy?" He then said: "By Allah, it is the supplication that I make for my Ummah in every prayer." (Al Bazzaar, Hasan)

The compassion Rasulallah ﷺ felt for others' suffering is evident in this Hadith: Abu Qatada(R.A) reported God's Messenger ﷺ as saying, "When I begin the prayer, I intend to make it long. But when I hear a child crying, I shorten the prayer, as I know his mother would suffer from his screams." (Bukhari, Mishkat al-Masabih 1130)

Narrated Ibn `Abbas(R.A): The Prophet ﷺ once came out to us and said, "Some nations were displayed before me. A Prophet would pass in front of me with one man, and another with two men, and another with a group of people. and another with nobody with him. Then I saw a great crowd covering the horizon and I wished that they were my followers, but it was said to me, 'This is Musa(A.S) and his followers.' Then it was said to me, 'Look" I looked and saw a big gathering with a large number of people covering the horizon. It was said, "Look this way and that way.' So, I saw a big crowd covering the horizon. Then it was said to me, "These are your followers, and among them, there are 70,000 who will enter Paradise without (being asked about their) accounts. " Then the people dispersed and the Prophet ﷺ did not tell who those 70,000 were. So, the companions of the Prophet ﷺ started talking about that and some of them said, "As regards us, we were born in the era of paganism, but then we believed in Allah and His Apostle ﷺ. We think, however, that these (70,000) are our offspring." That talk reached the Prophet ﷺ who said, "These (70,000) are the people who do not draw an evil omen from (birds) and do not get treated by branding themselves and do not treat with Ruqya, but put their trust (only) in their Lord." then 'Ukasha bin Muhsin got up and said, "O Allah's Messenger ﷺ! Am I one of those (70,000)?" The Prophet ﷺ said, "Yes." Then another person got up and said, "Am I one of them?" The Prophet ﷺ said, " 'Ukasha has anticipated you." (Sahih al-Bukhari 5752)

Anas bin Malik and Ibn Hazm said: "The Messenger of Allah ﷺ said: 'Allah, the Mighty and Sublime, enjoined fifty prayers upon my Ummah, and I came back with that until I passed by Musa, peace be upon him, who said: 'What has your Lord enjoined upon your Ummah?' I said: 'He has enjoined fifty prayers on them.' Musa(A.S) said to me: 'Go back to your Lord, the Mighty and Sublime, for your Ummah will not be able to do that.' So, I went back to my Lord, the Mighty and Sublime, and He reduced a portion of it. Then I came back to Musa(A.S) and told him, and he said: 'Go back to you Lord, for your Ummah will not be able to do that.' So, I went back to my Lord, the Mighty and Sublime, and He said: 'They are five (prayers) but they are fifty (in reward), and the Word that comes from Me cannot be changed.' I came back to Musa(A.S) and he said: 'Go back to your Lord.' I said: 'I feel too shy before my Lord, the Mighty and Sublime.'"

How blessed as the last Ummah we are; A great Prophet of Allah, Prophet Musa a.s, helped our Holy Prophet ﷺ to reduce our daily prayers from fifty to five. This is surely an example of the love and respect of all previous Prophets of Allah to the last Prophet of Allah ﷺ and his Ummah.

Abdullah bin Amr bin Al-'as(R.A) reported: The Prophet ﷺ recited the Words of Allah, the Exalted, and the Glorious, about Ibrahim ﷺ who said: "O my Rubb! They have led astray many among mankind. But whosoever follows me, he verily, is of me". (14:36) and those of 'Isa (Jesus) ﷺ who said: "If You punish them, they are Your slaves, and if You forgive them, verily, You, only You, are the All-Mighty, the All-Wise". (5:118). Then he ﷺ raised up his hands and said, "O Allah! My Ummah, my Ummah," and wept;

Allah, the Exalted, said: "O Jibril (Gabriel)! Go to Muhammad ﷺ and ask him: 'What makes you weep?" So Jibril came to him and asked him (the reason for his weeping) and the Messenger of Allah informed him what he had said (though Allah knew it well).

Upon this Allah said: "Jibril, go to Muhammad ﷺ and say: 'Verily, We will please you with regard to your Ummah and will never displease you". [Muslim]

Another Hadith that relieves us from the difficulties of the Day of the Judgement is the Dua of Intercession of our Holy Prophet ﷺ for his Ummah.

Abu Hurairah(R.A) narrated that the Messenger of Allah ﷺ said:

"Every Prophet has a (special) supplication which is answered. Verily, I have reserved mine as intercession for my Ummah, and it shall reach, if Allah wills, those of them who die, not associating anything with Allah(S.W.T)." (Jami` at-Tirmidhi 3602)

It is evident from the stated Hadiths that Rasulallah ﷺ reserves special favour for his ummah. In this worldly life, we should strive to strongly attach ourselves to the Qur'an's teachings and the Sunnah of our Holy Prophet ﷺ, and become practising Muslims, to receive this immense favour of Allah(S.W.T) on the Day of Judgement.

HOW TO SHOW OUR LOVE TO THE HOLY PROPHET ﷺ?
SENDING BLESSINGS ON RASULALLAH ﷺ

"Indeed, Allah showers His blessings upon the Prophet, and His angels pray for him.
O believers! Invoke Allah's blessings upon him, and salute him with worthy greetings of peace."
(Surah Al-Ahzab, V:56)

Durood-o-Salam is solely done for asking Allah(S.W.T) to bestow His Blessings and Mercy on His Messenger ﷺ in order to show one's reverence and gratitude for Rasulullah's ﷺ services to the Religion of Islam. It not only completes the Prophet's ﷺ right of honour but also results in getting many bounties and rewards from Allah, the Exalted, in this world and the hereafter.

Abdullah ibn Ma'sud(R.A) narrates that Sayyidina Rasulullah ﷺ said:

"On the day of Qiyamah, the person closest to me will be the one who has sent the most Durood unto me." (Tirmidhi)

Abdullah bin `Amr bin Al-`As(R.A) reported: I heard the Messenger ﷺ of Allah saying:

"Whoever supplicates Allah to exalt for me, Allah would exalt him ten times." (Muslim)

Friday is the most revered and blessed day of the week in Islam, which is even mentioned in the Holy Qur'an. This day encloses the greatest virtues in gaining the blessings of Allah through different modes of worship like Jummuah prayer and reciting Surah Kahf and other prayers like Durood Sharif.

The Messenger of Allah ﷺ said,

"On Fridays, send Durood abundantly on me, as it is presented before me." (Abu Dawud)

So, Salawat sent on the Holy Prophet ﷺ on the auspicious day of Friday results in great reward in the form of getting prominent near Rasulullah ﷺ as He receives them Himself.

As a true disciple of Islam, we need to feel affection for the Messenger ﷺ of Allah more than anything else in the world, and that right of Prophet ﷺ could only be fulfilled through adhering to His Sunnah and recalling and venerating His name all the time.

May Allah(S.W.T) place us among those who will be granted the love of Rasulullah ﷺ and be among those who will spread his enduring love to humanity. May we among those who spread love and not hate, spread peace and not conflict, spread unity and not division.

AMEEN

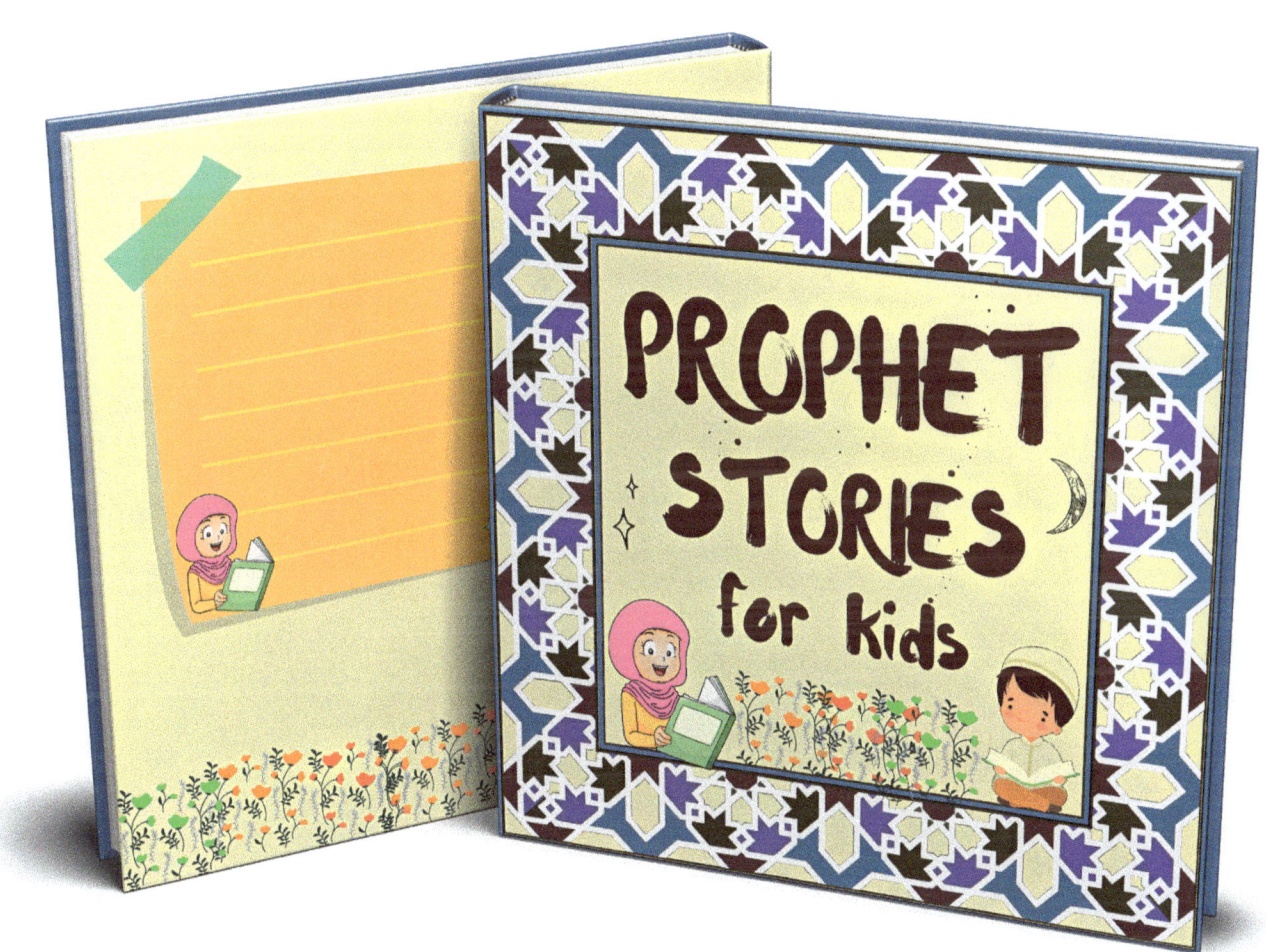

ISBN 978-1-990544-43-9

*Search ISBN on the retailer website

Premium Color Pages Hardcover

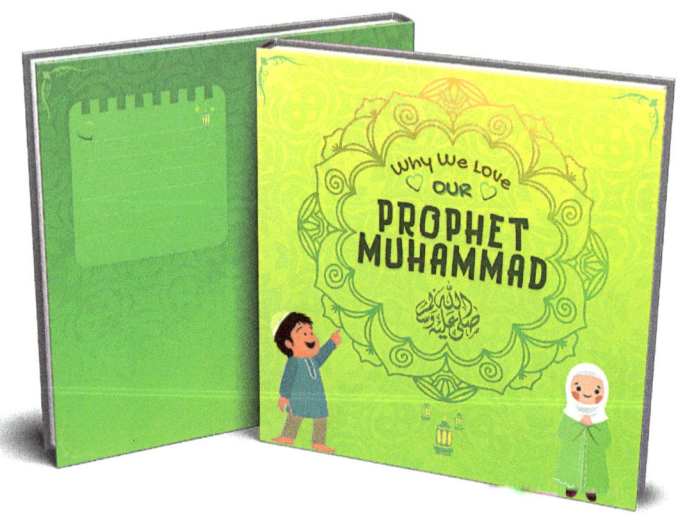

ISBN 978-1-990544-42-2

ISBN 978-1-990544-41-5

ISBN 978-1-990544-45-3

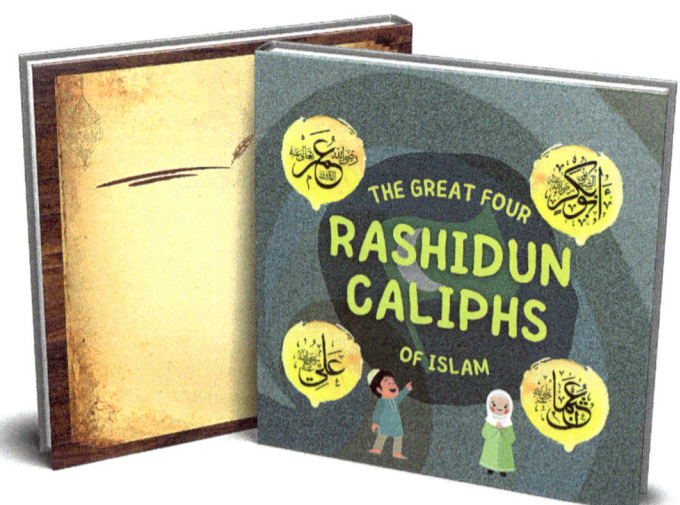

ISBN 978-1-990544-44-6

*Search ISBN on the retailer website